EIGHTH NOTE PUBLICATIONS

For Those Who Have Served

David Marlatt

Sounding very patriotic in nature *For Those Who Have Served* would make an ideal selection to be performed at a reflective event or simply to pay homage to the thousands of men and women who have served in the military or front line workers during times of crisis. The noble theme is first heard in a solo flugel horn before moving to a more full sonority. Another theme with a very different feel is introduced before the flugel horn sound brings this lyrical piece to peaceful conclusion.

Performance with a slideshow showing veterans or current service men and women would be a very appropriate addition and could be used at a Remembrance Day or Veteran's Day ceremony.

T0054410

David Marlatt (b. 1973) is an accomplished Canadian composer, arranger and publisher. He writes music for concert band, string orchestra and a wide variety of chamber groups. Since the creation of Eighth Note Publications in 1996, he has composed over 200 works and arranged more than 1100 pieces ranging from the Baroque era to the Romantic era. Mr. Marlatt primarily writes for the educational market where he is regularly commissioned by elementary schools and high schools in both Canada and the United States. He regularly makes guest appearances and conducts workshops with ensembles at schools, community groups and professional ensembles and adjudicates at both local and provincial festivals. In 2019 Mr. Marlatt received the Canadian Band Association's Canadian Composer Award for his contributions to wind band repertoire, an award which has only been given to six other composers since its inception.

*Please contact the composer if you require any further information about this piece
or his availability for commissioning new works and appearances.*

david@enpmusic.com

ISBN: 9781771577380
CATALOG NUMBER: BQ220506

COST: $15.00
DURATION: 2:45

DIFFICULTY RATING: Easy-Medium
Brass Quintet

www.enpmusic.com

FOR THOSE WHO HAVE SERVED

David Marlatt

© 2020 **EIGHTH NOTE PUBLICATIONS**
www.enpmusic.com

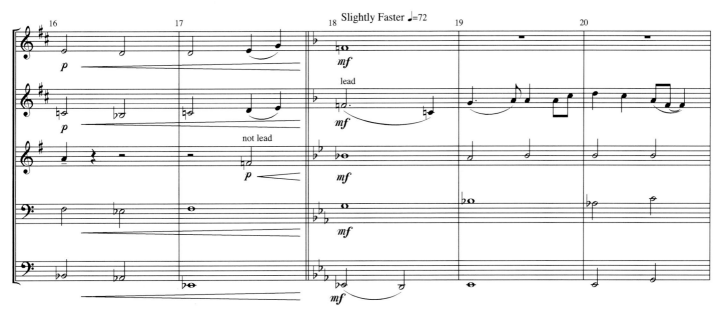

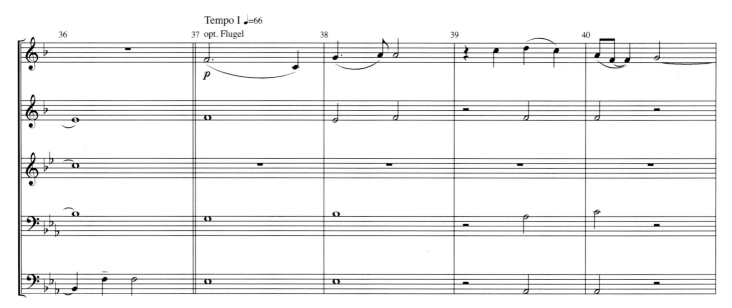

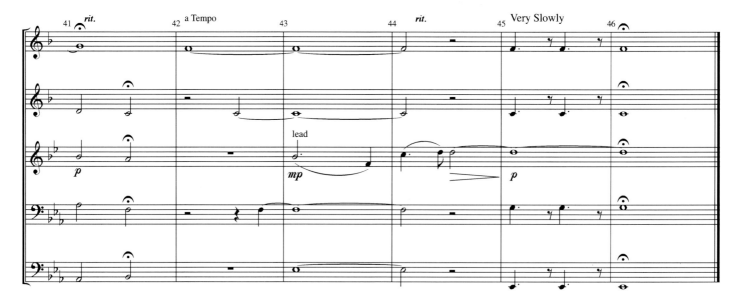

FOR THOSE WHO HAVE SERVED pg. 3

Bb Trumpet 1 and
Flugel horn

FOR THOSE WHO HAVE SERVED

David Marlatt

© 2020 EIGHTH NOTE PUBLICATIONS
www.enpmusic.com

Bb Trumpet 2

FOR THOSE WHO HAVE SERVED

David Marlatt

© 2020 EIGHTH NOTE PUBLICATIONS
www.enpmusic.com

F Horn

FOR THOSE WHO HAVE SERVED

David Marlatt

© 2020 EIGHTH NOTE PUBLICATIONS
www.enpmusic.com

Trombone

FOR THOSE WHO HAVE SERVED

David Marlatt

© 2020 EIGHTH NOTE PUBLICATIONS
www.enpmusic.com

Tuba

FOR THOSE WHO HAVE SERVED

David Marlatt

© 2020 EIGHTH NOTE PUBLICATIONS
www.enpmusic.com